Getting To Know...

Nature's Children

GUIDE

Pamela Hickman

PUBLISHER   Joseph R. DeVarennes
PUBLICATION DIRECTOR   Kenneth H. Pearson
MANAGING EDITOR   Valerie Wyatt
SERIES ADVISOR   Merebeth Switzer
SERIES CONSULTANT   Michael Singleton
CONSULTANTS   Ross James
                                   Kay McKeever
                                   Dr. Audrey N. Tomera

ADVISORS   Roger Aubin
                                   Robert Furlonger
                                   Gaston Lavoie

EDITORIAL SUPERVISOR   Jocelyn Smyth
PRODUCTION MANAGER   Ernest Homewood
PRODUCTION ASSISTANTS   Penelope Moir
                                   Brock Piper

EDITORS   Katherine Farris   Anne Minguet-Patocka
                 Sandra Gulland   Sarah Reid
                 Cristel Kleitsch   Cathy Ripley
                 Elizabeth MacLeod   Eleanor Tourtel
                 Pamela Martin   Karin Velcheff

PHOTO EDITORS   Bill Ivy
                                   Don Markle

DESIGN   Annette Tatchell
CARTOGRAPHER   Jane Davie
PUBLICATION ADMINISTRATION   Kathy Kishimoto
                                   Monique Lemonnier

ARTISTS   Marianne Collins   Greg Ruhl
                 Pat Ivy   Mary Theberge

This series is approved and recommended by the Federation of Ontario Naturalists.

Canadian Cataloguing in Publication Data

Hickman, Pamela.
  Guide and index

(Getting to know—nature's children; 26)
Supplement to: Getting to know—nature's children.
ISBN 0-7172-1945-3

1. Getting to know—nature's children—Indexes.
2. Zoology—North America—Juvenile literature—Indexes.
I. Title.   II. Series.

QL151.H53 1985   j591.97   C85-099669-4

Contents

Introduction

Children are fascinated by wildlife. Their innate enthusiasm and curiosity are tremendous resources that should not go untapped. Learning about wildlife and enjoying the natural environment are important parts of growing up. You can offer guidance and encouragement, share the learning process and help youngsters develop positive attitudes towards nature which they may carry for the rest of their life.

The *Nature's Children* Series was conceived as a way of building on a child's sense of wonder about wildlife. These books can serve as a key to open the door to a lifetime of discoveries. This volume is designed for further knowledge and to give you concrete suggestions for providing hands-on experiences. Nature study can be one of the most accessible and rewarding pastimes.

Contact with nature is not restricted to the wilderness camper or the rural land owner. An amazing variety of creatures thrive in urban areas if you know where to look and what to look for. Habitats may be as big as a backyard or local park, or as small as the leaf on a tree or a crack in the sidewalk. When it comes to wildlife, bigger is not necessarily better. Tiny creatures often have fascinating life cycles, social structures and physical characteristics, and they are often more accessible and easier to study than larger ones.

If you have the opportunity, you can try to create or improve wildlife habitats around your home. Using these suggestions for attracting and observing wildlife, you can increase contact with species, as well as awareness of the complex relationships between animals and their environment. As observation skills develop and familiarity with the local scene grows, the interdependence of living things becomes more visible and more easily comprehended. Seeing these interrelationships is one of the keys to understanding the intangible balance of nature.

In addition to building an understanding and appreciation of the natural environment, practical, hands-on activities are tremendously valuable in a child's learning process. Projects such as building bird houses or feeders provide opportunities for children to become actively involved in caring for wildlife. Learning about animals and then using this newly acquired knowledge to do something positive and constructive is complete education. The experience becomes meaningful and memorable.

Your encouragement can start youngsters on the road to adventure, hobbies and possibly even a career. Share these books with them. Learn together.

Developing Attitudes

*We do not inherit the earth from our forefathers; we
borrow it, for a short time, from our children.*

Anon.

This observation has been echoed by many individuals
who care about the future of our natural environment. It
implies a serious responsibility on behalf of the adult world to
pass on a healthy and diverse environment to the next
generation. We must try to hand over the best possible
environment, and it is our collective responsibility to ensure
that youth are prepared to accept this legacy.

With the recognition of this responsibility comes an
implicit need to educate our youth and inspire in them an
awareness and understanding of their environment. Planting
and nurturing an environmental ethic within a child is an
investment in the future of our environment. It can also be, for
the child, the beginning of a lifetime of appreciation and
enjoyment of nature.

Sparking a youngster's interest in the environment can
deepen your own experience too. First impressions can be the
basis for future enjoyment or indifference toward nature, so
make a child's first contact fun and rewarding. Young people
learn by example. Consequently, in many cases, your actions
speak louder than words. Put away your preconceptions about
things that wiggle and wriggle or creep and crawl. Pull out your
boots and jeans and start from scratch, like a child with
unspoiled curiosity.

Throughout your shared experiences, it is important to
reinforce your own values and attitudes towards the
environment. Your attitudes will be reflected in what you do

and will often turn up in the actions of young children. Respect for other living things should be emphasized in all activities, whether it means releasing a temporary pet, returning an overturned log to its original position or keeping your dog leashed in a park to avoid disturbing the local wildlife.

All wildlife deserves respect. Big or small, cute or ugly, each animal plays its role in a food web and contributes to the overall balance in its ecosystem. This delicate balance is so complex that scientists are still unable to predict the long term impact of an upset. When a species becomes extinct, it is no longer found anywhere in the world. The effect of this loss may be large or it may appear relatively insignificant—the problem is that nobody knows what will happen.

In many jurisdictions, legislation to protect endangered species—those on the edge of extinction—is in place. In addition, laws exist to prevent the over-harvesting of different species and ensure that viable populations are maintained. The ultimate goal, of course, is to rehabilitate those species currently in trouble, and prevent other species from suffering similar declines. The scientific management of wildlife is a growing field, becoming more accepted and necessary as humans continue to alter natural habitats. In our laws, as in our daily lives, it is important to remember that protection must not be restricted to the attractive or economically valuable species. Although it may be easier to feel sympathy for a baby rabbit than a snake, each one is important and merits our efforts to ensure its future survival.

Caring for a pet or nurturing an orphaned or injured animal can be a valuable lesson in respecting the rights of wild creatures. The desire to take in baby animals is understandable, but in almost all cases should be denied. Part of respecting wildlife involves understanding that young animals have the right to be raised in the wild by their mother and to live a free and natural life. If you take in an animal that has been injured, there is an implicit responsibility to prepare it for a return to the wild and release it when it is ready. These can be heart-tugging moments, but they are all part of the learning process.

Sometimes observations of wildlife turn up confusing or even negative experiences that must be handled delicately, but honestly. The killing of one animal by another is not a pleasant sight. It may elicit anger or fear from a child who does not understand the idea of predator-prey relationships. Each animal feeds on something (plant or animal) and is in turn fed on by other animals (except for a species at the top of the food chain, such as an eagle or bear). This system is designed to sustain viable populations which can maintain their numbers without depleting their resources. When predators are controlled, the balance is upset and everything suffers. For example, foxes feed on rabbits, among other things. No one likes the thought of a rabbit being killed and eaten by a fox, but this natural activity is important not only to the fox, but to the survival of the rabbit population as well. If foxes were prevented from killing rabbits, the number of rabbits would increase quickly and dramatically. With a major natural population control gone, there would soon be more rabbits than available food or habitat. When food ran out, many rabbits would starve and other might succumb to disease. In other words, if the predator-prey balance is upset, life is still lost, but to the detriment of both species.

Some wildlife can occasionally be a nuisance or a danger to people. Problems can range from squirrels in the attic to bears in the campsite. Understanding why animals behave as they do can help you to avoid problems as well as to handle those that may occur. Children need to be aware of the possible dangers that some wildlife represents, but they should not fear all wildlife. A knowledge of animal habits and responses under stress can go a long way to prevent unpleasant experiences. Even so, if you plan to take children into wild areas, you should discuss the proper way of handling potentially serious wildlife encounters.

Knowing how to experience wildlife in its many forms can create new opportunities which add enjoyment and depth to life. Teaching children how to interpret their natural surroundings by exercising their own senses can open doors to new insights. Relating to nature as a part of it, not as an observer only, will reinforce the concept of our inescapable role in the overall balance.

Living with Wildlife

Contact with wildlife occurs under many different circumstances and for a variety of reasons. Most contacts are positive, but problems may arise in certain situations. Living with wildlife involves minimizing human impact, reducing potential problems by taking precautions, understanding and respecting an animal's natural instincts, and knowing how to cope when conflict arises.

Children are endlessly curious and they are fascinated by wildlife. They want to learn about animals, see them and get close to them. A nest of fluffy, newly hatched ducklings is an irresistible sight. A child's first instinct is often a desire to hold one of the babies, and then to take it home. Almost all baby animals look cute and cuddly. They stir up the urge to protect, nurture and care for something. Denying a child's requests to adopt one of these finds is often difficult, but handled delicately, it can turn into an important lesson.

When a nest or other nursery site is discovered and there is evidence of parental care, observe at a distance. If the opportunity is available, let children watch the mother with her young. Observe her caring for her babies; cleaning them, feeding them, and keeping them warm and safe. Point out the special things that only a natural mother can offer. Discuss what would happen if you took one of the babies away. You could never duplicate the baby's natural environment or know all of the things that its natural mother does for it every day. Most young animals taken from the wild by well-intentioned but inexperienced people do not survive. Even if it did live, the baby would grow up without any others of its own kind and would not be taught the necessary skills for survival. Explain that people do not have the right to deny these basic living conditions to other species. Wild animals belong in their natural habitat where they can live and reproduce with as little human interference as possible.

In addition to the moral reasons for leaving wildlife in the wild, there are many legal reasons too. There are laws that prohibit the killing or injuring of particular species, and also laws that forbid the collection or possession of some species. Legislation protecting wild animals varies from one state, province or country to another. Find out what wildlife protection laws exist in your area and discuss them.

Generally speaking, wild animals avoid humans. There are, however, a growing number of exceptions to this rule. Some animals are adapting remarkably well to the human environment and can be found living and multiplying even in large urban areas. The food and shelter opportunities afforded by human communities attract a number of animals. These animals are known as opportunists—they take advantage of suitable living conditions and move right in without an invitation. Common urban species include raccoons, squirrels and skunks, and there is no doubt that they can be nuisances. The best way to avoid problems is to eliminate the opportunities. Keeping garbage tightly contained, barricading all exterior access points into your attic, and especially not leaving hand-outs, can all reduce the likelihood of an invasion.

If you do get squirrels in your attic or raccoons in your chimney, there are practical, humane solutions. First of all, remember that the animal is merely claiming squatter's rights— as far as anyone knows, it is not a malicious vandal. Observe the uninvited guests carefully for one or two days to determine how many are there. Also try to find out when they go out for food.

Raccoons, for instance, tend to go out in the evening. Wait until they are all out of their headquarters, and then seal off all entry holes with hardware cloth. Use heavy wire mesh to cover the chimney. If a mother is nursing, however, she will leave her young inside during her evening prowls. Do not seal the young inside as they will die. If you can wait, the best solution is to postpone the eviction until the young are weaned and accompanying their mother on her outings. Other less successful alternatives involve making the new home undesirable by spreading mothballs around, causing excessive noise or shining bright lights on the invaders. As a last resort, call a professional pest remover. Find out what methods are used before agreeing to the services—like it or not, the welfare of these animals is still your responsibility.

Garden raiders, such as rabbits and raccoons, can also cause frustration. Try fencing off your garden or suspending a string of bright lights over it to intimidate the freeloaders.

Sometimes people or pets run into problems with animals quite by accident. Unknowingly, you can aggravate a species whose instincts tell it to defend itself—usually to your detriment. Bee and wasp stings are often the result of an unwitting disturbance, as is the unpleasant spray from a skunk. However hard you may try to avoid such an occurrence, accidents can, and do, happen. It is important to know how to react, for everyone's safety and peace of mind.

For instance, children may develop an irrational fear of bees after being stung. Although understanding the bee's natural instinct to defend itself or its hive does nothing to ease the discomfort, it can put the whole incident in a new perspective, easing a child's fear of an unprovoked assault. Bee and wasp stings can be painful and may swell up. If a person is stung in the mouth, medical attention is advised since the tongue and throat may swell and make breathing difficult or impossible. Allergic reactions are rare, but can be dangerous. If you are unsure about an individual's hypersensitivity to stings, watch closely for excessive swelling or other side effects. If you have any doubts about an allergic response, see a doctor immediately. People with known hypersensitivity should carry an insect bite kit containing antihistamine tablets and a syringe of adrenalin. They should also wear a medic-alert tag. If you are sure that the victim is not allergic, wash the area around the sting and apply an ice pack to reduce the swelling. In addition, antihistamine cream can be applied effectively, as can a thick paste made of baking soda and water. To reduce contact with wasps, avoid feeding them unwittingly. Keep garbage tightly contained and remove food scraps, meat-based pet foods and rotting fruits from your property.

Running into a skunk is a memorable experience, but not a pleasant one. Even when the animal leaves, its "spirit" can linger for a long time. To de-skunk your clothes, try washing them in a mixture of ammonia and water. As for yourself, wash with tomato juice and then soap and water. If spray has entered your eyes, rinse them thoroughly with water only.

Pets may also be the victims of negative encounters with wildlife. Sprayings by skunks and run-ins with porcupines are two of the most common problem situations. Keeping your pet on a leash or in a confined area will save it from needless trouble and possible injury. It may also help to protect the local wildlife. Dogs running loose can attack and kill many small species such as chipmunks, birds and woodchucks, and they have also been known to kill larger animals such as deer or young moose by running them to exhaustion in deep snow. Controlling your pet benefits everyone.

If your pet does get sprayed you will probably know about it in a hurry. To get rid of the odor, bathe your pet in tomato juice. After the juice has dried, brush it out. Repeat the whole process as often as necessary. If your dog arrives home with a hide full of quills or has quills inside its mouth, consult a veterinarian. If only a few quills are present, you can probably take care of the situation. Porcupine quills are very painful and can be dangerous if not removed quickly. The tiny barbs on the quills make them difficult to remove and sometimes cause them to work their way in deeper. In addition, quills are filled with air. As the dogs body heat warms the trapped air, the quill swells. By clipping the end of the quill with scissors, you can reduce the air pressure and swelling, making the quill easier to remove. Once the quill is clamped, pull it out using strong pliers.

What to Do If . . .

In addition to wildlife encounters on your home ground, there are occasions when problems arise in the wild. People seeking a wilderness experience may be perceived by an animal as encroaching on its territory. Under certain circumstances some wild creatures defend their territory. This reaction can range from a harmless warning noise, such as the scolding of a jay, the slap of a beaver's tail or the rattling of a snake, to the extreme cases of assault.

Animals can also be more aggressive at certain times of year. Mating season is often a time when the males of a species are setting up territories, defending boundaries and challenging all threats, real or perceived. When a female is with young she may feel threatened by human presence. Her natural instinct may be to flee with her young or to distract you away from the babies. It may also be to remove the threat by attacking.

When you are planning to visit a wild area, find out what potentially dangerous animals may be encountered and learn how to avoid disturbing them unnecessarily. Make sure everyone is told of your findings. It is also wise to set some basic rules, such as no wandering off alone, and always wearing a loud whistle or carrying a signalling device. In case you do run into a problem, ways of dealing with various situations should be discussed in advance.

Different animals may respond differently in the same situation. It is therefore important that you know what to expect from each species. Some of the most serious wildlife encounters, representing a very small incidence rate when compared to the number of people visiting the wilds, involve Black Bears, Grizzly Bears and snakes.

Black Bears

The most common meetings between Black Bears and people involve human food or garbage. Most encounters end without injury or with only minor personal injury, but they can cause considerable damage to equipment such as tents and coolers.

In many parks, Black Bears have learned to beg food from tourists—or steal it if necessary. The problem is often aggravated by poorly managed garbage dumps, ignorant people giving hand-outs to wild bears or careless storage of food while in bear country. Never feed wildlife—it is cruel and unnecessary. Animals that learn to associate people with food, especially in campgrounds, become nuisances. In the case of nuisance bears, they are often captured and translocated, and in some cases, they must be destroyed.

When camping, you should do your part to avoid attracting bears and other potential nuisance animals, such as raccoons, squirrels and skunks. Food is the number one lure for wildlife. It should be stored in sealed containers (plastic or metal) to eliminate odors and placed in the trunk of your car— *never* in your tent. Food-contaminated garbage, such as cans and meat-wrappings, may also draw unwanted attention and should be treated in the same way. If you find garbage at the campsite when you arrive, quickly clean it up and store it in your trunk or in the animal-proof containers often provided. You will be doing yourself a favor, as well as setting a good example.

Although raccoons or Red Squirrels may appear harmless in comparison to a bear, they are very adept at raiding food packs, ripping apart flimsy containers such as styrofoam, and seeking out unsealed food packages. Your camping experience can be ruined if one of these animals destroys your food supply. In addition, all spills, particularly sweet substances like sugar, should be thoroughly cleaned up so that they will not be a temptation, especially to problem wasps.

Black Bears rarely attack because of a sudden encounter with people. It is always safest, however, to keep your distance and go out of your way to avoid a bear. There are four basic reasons why a Black Bear may show signs of aggression. The following chart lists the probable cause along with a suggested reaction.

Cause	*Suggested Reaction*
You are too close and the bear wants more space.	• back away and keep your eye on the bear at all times (once you are far enough you should no longer pose a threat and the bear should leave); • if you are near shelter, slowly make your way there but do not turn your back on the animal;
It wants your food.	• give up your food—it is not worth fighting for; • loud noises are often successful in discouraging a bear from returning;
It is a mother defending her cubs.	• play dead (once the bear thinks the threat to her cubs is removed she will take them away);

Predation—black bears have *very occasionally* stalked and attacked people during the day to prey upon them (this is more likely to occur in remote areas, where bears have had little association with people).

- fight back using any available weapon, even a rock, and then try to escape to shelter;
- black bears can climb trees quite easily, so this is usually not a successful escape route.

Grizzly Bears

As with the Black Bear, many Grizzly encounters involve food. When backpacking in Grizzly country do not leave food or garbage in accessible areas. Seal it in plastic bags or containers to reduce odors and hoist it between two trees. Never put food in your tent. When cooking, set your fire downwind, well away from your tent, and try to avoid getting food odors on your clothes. When hiking, try to make regular, loud noises to warn any bears in the area of your presence. If warned in time a bear will usually avoid you.

If you take these simple precautions, you are unlikely to catch more than a far-off glimpse of a Grizzly. However, it is worth being specially cautious if there may be young about, or around berry patches. A Grizzly may attack if surprised, especially a mother with cubs.

In the event that you do surprise a Grizzly, you have a number of choices.

1. If the bear has not attacked and there is a tree nearby, climb up it as high as possible. Although Grizzlies cannot climb trees very well, they are incredibly fast, so be sure that you can make it to the tree before the bear does. Stay in the tree until the bear has been gone for at least 15 minutes, then leave quickly and report the incident to authorities.

2. If the bear has not attacked and you are in the open, stand your ground or slowly back away. Talk to the bear and try to let it know that you are not a threat. Avoid staring directly at the bear (this may be perceived as threatening), but watch it closely.

3. If the bear attacks and there is a nearby tree you could climb, drop something to distract its attention. Only drop your pack as a last resort, as it may provide needed protection. Even a few seconds delay in attack can be vital.

4. If the bear attacks and you are in the open, play dead. Never fight a Grizzly unless you have a proper weapon. Resistance only aggravates the assault, whereas playing dead may cause the bear to leave.

Snakes

Snakes have been maligned for centuries and they are still the subject of much misunderstanding. For instance, many people think a snake is being aggressive when it flicks its tongue in and out. The snake's tongue, however, is a harmless sensory organ which helps it to smell its surroundings.

The majority of snakes are not poisonous, and all snakes will do their utmost to flee from anything they perceive as a threat. If grabbed or stepped upon, however, they will do what any animal would do—defend themselves. Since they have lots of pointy teeth, even non-poisonous snakes may give a painful bite if handled. Standard treatment of a non-venomous snake bite involves cleaning the wound with an antiseptic solution to avoid possible infection.

Although harmless snakes far outnumber the poisonous ones, being able to recognize a venomous snake can be very important. There are four types of poisonous snakes in North

America: rattlesnakes, copperheads, moccasins and coral snakes. The first three types belong to the pit viper group. The most reliable physical trait by which to identify them is the pair of pits between the eye and the nostril. These pits are heat sensitive and allow a snake to sense its prey. Keep in mind that a snake's venom is designed for catching food, not attacking people.

Rattlesnakes are the most common poisonous snake in North America. They are found in several parts of the United States and in southern Canada. Under normal circumstances rattlesnakes, like all snakes, will retreat from people, but some precautions are still advised. When in rattlesnake country, wear protective trousers. Always carry a flashlight at night and feel about with a stick before reaching into bushes or collecting firewood. If you do come across a rattlesnake, keep still. Listen carefully to find out its location and then slowly move away in the opposite direction. It will not chase or follow you.

Rattlesnakes are not considered aggressive. Normally, they will rattle to warn and frighten away predators, but they may not, particularly if they are suddenly stepped on. If bitten, get to the nearest hospital or doctor for antivenin treatment. This applies to a pet as well. If you are in a remote area, a snake bite kit may be your best friend. These kits contain suction devices, scalpel, tourniquet and an antiseptic solution. The suction devices can remove some of the venom if applied directly to the fang punctures. A properly applied tourniquet can prevent the spread of venom. Place the tourniquet between the bite and the victim's heart. It should be tight enough to compress soft tissues but not so tight it stops blood circulation. The victim should move as little as possible, and be carried to help. Heat should not be applied to the bitten area, nor should any alcohol be given to the victim. Both of these activities will increase blood circulation, facilitating the spread of venom.

Never pick up a recently killed rattlesnake because its nerve reflexes enable it to bite for some time after death.

* * *

When thousands of people interact with wild animals every year, it is inevitable that *occasional* problems will occur. Sometimes an animal is a nuisance, sometimes a threat. Whatever the situation, if you understand the potential for problems and take steps to avoid them, you can minimize the risks of a negative encounter. Respecting the rights of other animals to share this earth is fundamental to learning to live with them.

Caring for Orphaned or Injured Wildlife

Seeing a baby animal without its parents nearby arouses feelings of sympathy and a desire to protect the apparently abandoned or orphaned creature. Restrain yourself—in most cases the parents are close by. A mother deer or a mother rabbit will leave her baby well hidden while she goes off to feed. Because the baby will not move from its spot, it may appear abandoned. Almost certainly, however, the mother is taking good care of it in her own way. Some birds, such as owls, woodpeckers and all songbirds, leave the nest before they can fly or care for themselves. Although they may appear abandoned, the parents are probably watching from nearby, as they gather food or care for other young.

Occasionally you may come across a nest or a nestling that has been blown from a tree. A nest should be replaced in the tree as high as possible. If you find a nestling, put it back in its nest. If it is shaking with cold, warm it up in your hands first. Place your hand over the nest to simulate darkness. This calms the bird and causes it to settle into the nest better. The commonly held theory that adult birds will abandon young that have been touched by humans is not true. Adult birds may, however, abandon a nest if it is disturbed during construction or early in the incubation period.

Taking in an Orphan
If you are certain that a young bird has been abandoned or orphaned, take it out of immediate danger, provide shelter, warmth and food, and try to contact an animal care expert. If you cannot get immediate help you will have to do your best. Be prepared—young birds require almost constant attention day and night and are very difficult to care for properly. Here are a few suggestions to assist you.

Housing

House the bird in a berry box or similar container with a lining of shredded paper towels or tissues. Keep this substitute nest away from direct sunlight and drafts. Since young birds cannot maintain their body temperature before their feathers are well grown, you will need to provide a source of heat. Place the box on a heating pad (at a low setting) or suspend a light bulb overhead. Very young birds with few or no feathers will require a temperature of about 32° C (95° F). Try to maintain a temperature of around 27° C (80° F) for nestlings that are well covered with down.

Feeding

Like a human baby, baby animals can be fed formula. For young birds, mix up a supply of water, milk, egg yolks, pablum and vitamin drops. Combine the egg yolks with small amounts of water and milk and steam for 10 minutes. Thicken the mixture with pablum and add a few vitamin drops. Using an eye dropper, place food deep in the bird's throat. Very young birds should be fed every 15 minutes. Birds with feathers may only need food once an hour. Young birds should not be given water.

Wild birds should be returned to their natural habitat as soon as their tail feathers grow in. You must not forget that they are not pets. In some jurisdictions there are laws against keeping wild birds or mammals. A permit may be required even to nurse an injured owl back to health.

Very few animals that have been hand-reared are successfully re-introduced to the wild. A young mammal, such as a squirrel, that has been orphaned or abandoned is usually best left to try to cope in its natural environment. Interfere only if it is obviously starving or in immediate danger, in which case remove it to safety and contact an animal care expert. If you choose to raise it, feed it a warm mixture of one part evaporated milk to one part water every four hours, day and night. Holding the animal upright, use an eyedropper for feeding and try not to get the formula in its nose. Place the young squirrel in a ventilated box on top of a heating pad (set on low). When it is capable of feeding by itself, offer bits of raw vegetables, sunflower seeds and nuts, and a water supply. You should also supply sticks or pieces of wood on which to gnaw. As the squirrel develops, provide an exercise wheel, sold in pet stores, and later let it go outside.

Dealing with Injuries

There are many natural hazards facing wildlife every day and, consequently, animals can be injured in a number of ways. Seeing an animal in difficulty can be very upsetting, especially to children. Unless you are trained in animal care, an injured bird or mammal is very difficult to treat. Your best move is to seek professional help. An injured bird may already be traumatized, so handle it as little as possible. Gently herd it into a cardboard box or cover it with a jacket and carefully pick it up. Take it to an animal care expert, such as a veterinarian, as soon as possible. For emergency care, feed an adult bird a mixture of moistened canned dog food and hard-boiled egg. Supply a shallow dish of water as well.

If you find a bird that has hit a window and stunned itself, take it indoors and put it in a covered box. It will usually recover after a few hours and you can release it. To prevent this problem, suspend aluminum strips in front of the window or put up a silhouette of a raptor, such as a hawk, to scare birds away from the glass. Hawk silhouettes are easily made and can be a good project for a child. Find a picture of a hawk, eagle or other bird of prey, preferably in flight. Trace the picture onto a piece of paper and color the bird solidly black. Cut out the silhouette and hang it from the window frame.

Injured mammals should be taken to a veterinarian for expert care.

Wildlife as Pets

As a general rule, wildlife should be left in the wild. Most wild animals do not make good pets, and it is almost impossible to duplicate their natural habitat indoors, especially for a prolonged period. There are times, however, when briefly adopting a wildlife "pet" can be a rewarding and educational experience for a child, stimulating a life-long interest in nature.

Many children are instinctive collectors. When out on a ramble, it is wise to check their pockets before heading home—a wide variety of "hitchhikers" can be collected by enthusiastic young naturalists! In most cases, they should be returned to their natural habitat. However, the time may be right to launch a new kind of wildlife experience, and there are animals that make very good *temporary* pets. The responsibility of looking after and raising such a pet can help children develop a respect and understanding for other creatures. This can be an excellent base on which to build a sound environmental ethic.

The most important decision will be choosing the best pet. There are a lot of factors to consider, so take your time and choose carefully. A rushed or uninformed decision can not only prove fatal to the animal in question, but may destroy a child's initial enthusiasm. You should know something about an animal before attempting to adopt it. Some creatures, such as poisonous snakes, or aggressive animals such as Snapping Turtles, are potentially dangerous and are not recommended. Although this may seem obvious, many docile-seeming animals can give painful bites or give off unpleasant odors when disturbed or handled. Another consideration must be one of legality. In many states and provinces there is legislation which prohibits the collection or possession of certain native species.

Check with local wildlife authorities before taking a pet from the wild. These officials may also be able to provide some good advice to help you choose an appropriate species.

In general, small animals take up less space, eat less and make better pets. Consider the type of habitat that your new friend will require. It is vital that the pet's new environment resemble the natural one as closely as possible. Do not ignore insects either—they can make excellent pets as they often have a short life cycle which can be easily observed.

Once your decision is made, find out as much as you can before acquiring the animal. You will need to know its specific habitat requirements: wet or dry, warm or cool, light or dark. The type of food needed is also very important—some fish, for example, eat only live food, which can be very inconvenient and might prove impossible. In addition, some knowledge regarding the animal's life cycle is necessary, since its requirements may change from one life stage to another. For instance, a tadpole lives in water, but an adult frog or toad needs some dry land as well. Whatever your choice, prepare the container and some food before your pet arrives.

Following are three examples of animals—frogs, butterflies and ants—that can make good pets on a temporary basis. All three are represented in the Nature's Children Series, and can be read about in more detail. Remember: children must realize that, just like a cat or dog, a wild pet is a serious responsibility as well as a lot of fun.

Frogs
Common inhabitants of marshes, ponds and swamps, frogs continue to capture the attention and hearts of children of all ages. With a few guidelines on collecting, housing and feeding these smooth-skinned amphibians, you can discover how frogs live, feed and mature from an egg, through the tadpole stage, to the familiar adult.

To start at the beginning, use a kitchen strainer to collect some frog's eggs from a nearby wetland in the spring. The jelly-like, floating masses are made up of hundreds to thousands of eggs, so you will not need very much. Be sure to collect some of the natural water and aquatic plants to place in the aqua-terrarium (see instructions on building an aqua-terrarium). The eggs hatch about two weeks after they are laid. By looking at your specimens through a lens you can tell their approximate age. If an egg is about 50 percent black and 50 percent white, then it is freshly laid. At two to three days old, the egg is black all over, and at a week the egg takes on a dumbbell shape. Just before hatching, the forms of a head and tail can be discerned.

When the eggs hatch, keep a few tadpoles and return the others to their original habitat. The tadpoles, or polliwogs, go through a number of physical changes in a relatively short time. It is a good idea for children to keep a diary beside the aqua-terrarium for making notes on the daily activities and transformations. A hand lens will provide the chance to see otherwise invisible changes. At first, the tadpole's body is bulging with yolk and three pairs of external gills can be seen. Later on, the eyes and mouth form and the external gills are replaced by gill slits and internal gills. When the mouth has formed, set up a daily feeding schedule, including algae, boiled or wilted lettuce (not spinach), small pieces of hard-boiled egg or raw liver. Uneaten food should be removed each day.

As the tadpole matures, hind legs will appear first, followed by the front legs. At this stage, your pet will need some floating bark or wood on which to climb. When it starts gulping air at the water's surface, it is ready to climb out onto land. Now the baby frog will not eat because it is absorbing the nutrients which are stored in its tail, which gets shorter and shorter and eventually disappears. When this happens, the task of feeding your frog becomes more involved. A general diet of worms, insects and other small invertebrates, such as sowbugs or spiders, is recommended for an adult frog. You are advised to release the mature frog to its original habitat within a few days. It is important not to forget that your temporary pet is still a wild creature that will have a better chance of survival in its natural environment.

This whole experience will take an average of two months from egg to adult frog, with some exceptions depending on the species. Be forewarned, however, that Bullfrog tadpoles take two to three years to mature!

Building an Aqua-Terrarium

This type of container combines the necessary aquatic and terrestrial conditions for rearing a frog.

Materials
- ☐ aquarium tank—30 cm x 30 cm x 60 cm (12 in. x 12 in. x 24 in.) or larger
- ☐ screen cover for tank
- ☐ small stones
- ☐ aquatic plants
- ☐ earth
- ☐ moss
- ☐ pond water (not tap water)
- ☐ coarse sand or gravel
- ☐ pieces of wood or bark

Method
1. Pile small stones to a height of about 8 cm (3 in.) at one end of the tank.
2. Add aquatic plants and earth on top of the stones.

3. Place coarse sand or gravel over the earth and cover with moss.
4. Fill the tank with pond water, level with the bottom of the plants.
5. Cover the tank with a screen (a glass cover may not allow enough oxygen in).
6. Place bits of floating wood or bark in the water when the tadpoles' legs appear.
7. Keep the tank at temperatures between 18-24° C (64-70° F) and avoid strong sun, dry heat and drafts.

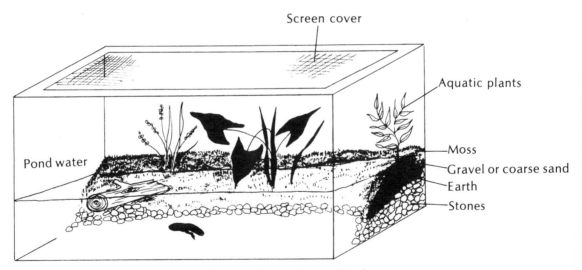

Screen cover

Aquatic plants

Pond water

Moss
Gravel or coarse sand
Earth
Stones

Aquarium 60 cm x 30 cm x 30 cm (24 in. x 12 in. x 12 in.)

AQUA-TERRARIUM

Butterflies

The grace and beauty of the varied, colorful butterflies are a delight to all observers. Whether sipping nectar from their favorite flowers, sailing on a breeze or warming up on a sunny rock, adult butterflies brighten the landscape and are among the best-liked members of our insect world.

One of the most popular and widely distributed North American butterflies is the Monarch. Readily recognized by many children, it just seems to appear at a certain time each year, with few questions asked. But the story of egg to adult is almost as unbelievable as the transformation itself. Raising a Monarch can be a relatively easy, short-term project for children—one that they are not likely to forget. As with the frog, the experience of raising a Monarch from egg to adult stage provides a complete picture of the creature's life cycle and unravels many mysteries unimagined by a child.

The adult Monarch lays its eggs on milkweed plants in early summer. Check under the leaves for a single, tiny, pale greenish-yellow egg. There are usually no more than three eggs on the same plant. Collect a few milkweed plants with eggs and place them in a large insect cage, as shown in the illustration. After five or six days, a tiny white caterpillar will emerge from each egg. (If you are unable to locate any eggs, you can start the rearing process from the caterpillar stage.)

Monarch caterpillars are very fussy eaters and will eat only the leaves of their host plant, the milkweed. The secret to success is to have a fresh, constant supply of milkweed leaves. A store of leaves in an airtight container with a bit of water can last from a week to ten days. Although the caterpillar starts off quite small, it grows rapidly. So would you if you ate day and night for two to three weeks! To allow for growth, the caterpillar molts several times and even eats its shed skin. The characteristic black, yellow and white tiger-striped colors develop gradually, leaving its caretakers with a very attractive, if voracious, pet.

From about the end of the second week, watch the caterpillar daily so that you notice when it stops eating and starts crawling restlessly around the cage. At this point it has finished growing. Within a day or two it will crawl to the top of the cage, spin a silken thread, attach itself upside down to it and hang in the shape of a J. Unseen by the human eye, there is a tremendous amount of activity taking place inside the caterpillar, and within a day the magic unfolds. With some luck (and patience) you can witness this fascinating event. The J-formation straightens out and slowly, the caterpillar sheds its skin for the last time. What is left behind is a plump, colorless chrysalis. Once dry, however, more magic takes place and the chrysalis takes on the shape and color of a jewel. Like an emerald pendant adorned with gold, the chrysalis hangs for 12 to 15 days. Although there appears to be no activity—the pupa, as this third stage in the butterfly's life cycle is called, does not eat or move—truly amazing changes are going on undercover. Towards the end of this period, excitement and anticipation mount as the chrysalis skin becomes transparent, revealing butterfly wings inside. For many youngsters it is truly a miracle.

A close watch should be kept so that the moment of emergence is not missed. First the chrysalis darkens, then the bottom splits open, and finally a beautiful winged creature bursts out. Now the exercises begin. Crinkled and wet, the butterfly stretches its legs, pumps fluid into its brilliant orange and black wings and coils and uncoils its long tongue. After it dries, the successfully reared pet will be ready for its maiden flight. Open the cage and let the butterfly test its wings. It will be content to rest on a plant in a sunny window for a day or two. Feed it two or three times a day, placing a drop of sugar or honey and water on your finger and allowing the butterfly to suck it up. After a couple of days, release the adult in the same area in which the eggs were found. Thus, the intricate and almost magical life cycle of the Monarch is complete.

Building an Insect Cage
Although many complicated designs exist, this simple cage can be easily constructed by a child, using few materials.

Materials
☐ window screening
☐ two round, straight-sided cake pans
☐ jar with lid (with holes punched through lid)
☐ water
☐ needle and thread

Method
1. Cut the screening to the desired height and sew the raw edges to form a cylinder.
2. Place the cylinder between the cake pans, as shown.
3. Place the food plant (milkweed for the Monarch), with eggs, in a jar of water. Force the stems through holes in the lid.
4. Place the jar in the cage.

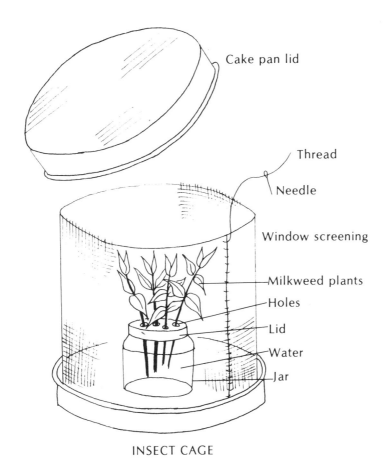

Cake pan lid

Thread

Needle

Window screening

Milkweed plants

Holes

Lid

Water

Jar

INSECT CAGE

Ants at Work

Ants are a large and widely distributed group of insects with a
complex social structure that has long intrigued professionals
and amateurs alike. Children are usually familiar with the
common ants found in lawns, cracks in the sidewalks and other
easily observable areas. But most ants spend much of their lives
in extensive underground tunnels, so many of their daily
activities go unseen. Creating an ant colony at home gives
children a special opportunity to watch, learn and discover.

In nature, ant colonies vary in size from dozens to thousands of individuals. Each colony has a queen (sometimes more than one), workers and males. The queen is the largest and most important member of the colony since she lays all the eggs.

Not all ants are alike, and some care should be taken to choose the right species for your colony. There are two major families of ants in North America: those with stinging females, including fire ants and harvester ants; and those with females that do not sting, including carpenter ants, mound-building ants and field ants. The latter group is to be preferred, for obvious reasons. You should also be aware that most ants will bite if disturbed, and some will even give off an unpleasant odor.

In order to get the best results from an ant colony, avoid handling any of the ants, ensure that the colony is securely sealed and observe the colony with as little disturbance as possible. With proper care, the colony will set up its passageways and follow its normal, organized regime right in front of your eyes.

Setting Up an Ant Colony
The following will enable you to construct a simplified version of an ant colony, suitable for young children.

Materials
☐ trowel
☐ large glass jar covered with a fine mesh screen
☐ elastic band
☐ soft, black earth
☐ black cloth or paper
☐ food for colony—sugar, honey, bits of meat and bread crumbs

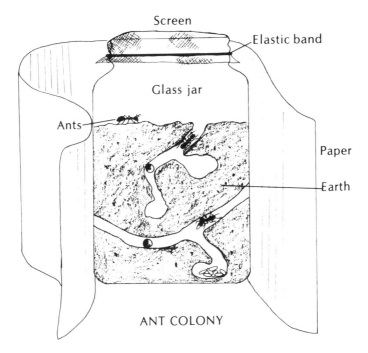

Screen

Elastic band

Glass jar

Ants

Paper

Earth

ANT COLONY

Method

1. Fill the jar three-quarters full with earth.
2. Locate a suitable ant colony and dig it up, using the trowel. Try to find the queen ant and place her in the jar with two to three hundred workers.
3. Cover the mouth of the jar with a screen, secured by an elastic band.
4. Cover the outside of the jar, up to the level of dirt, with black cloth or paper. This will keep the light out, simulating life underground.
5. Feed the ants daily.
6. In order to view the ants at work, remove the black cloth or paper for short intervals. You should be able to see their tunnels and chambers running down the sides of the jar.
7. When you have tired of the ant colony, return the ants to their original location.

Attracting Wildlife

Whether you live in an urban area with a small backyard, or own a large rural acreage or farm, you can enhance your property to increase its value as a habitat for wildlife. With some careful planning and effort, you can achieve an attractive array of trees, shrubs and flowers that will beautify your surroundings and provide functional shelter and food for wildlife as well. Not only will you be helping to maintain or increase local wildlife populations, but you will also benefit from their regular visits to your locale.

Children can get actively involved in this project and can learn a great deal from the experience. They can learn what local wildlife populations exist, what types of habitat different species prefer, what foods different species eat and where they may be found. Nor will the learning process end once you have succeeded in attracting some wildlife visitors. There are so many questions: what does a particular bird look like? can you identify it? where does it nest? how does it defend its territory? what is the nest made of? how many young does it raise? how are the young cared for? when do the young leave the nest? what does it eat? what are its predators? does it stay around all year? what does its song sound like? does it have more than one song? . . .

The educational value of this activity is not limited to observational skills. Helping wildlife and understanding the need to provide suitable habitat is the beginning to appreciating our natural surroundings and realizing that they cannot, and should not, be taken for granted. As human populations grow and spread, even young children can begin to see the encroachment of new housing on once vacant meadows, the loss of natural areas to roads, schools, shopping centers and industries. This loss of habitat results in a decline in numbers and in the diversity of species in a local area. Although some losses are inevitable, helping to minimize the impact of these losses teaches a child a sense of responsibility for the environment. Learning to care for and help even the common species reinforces the idea that all creatures deserve a place to live and grow.

First efforts to attract wildlife might well focus on birds, butterflies and moths.

Birds

The three major requirements for good bird habitat are: food, nesting sites, and protection from predators and bad weather. Basically, you are limited only by your geographical area, which affects the type of plantings that will succeed, and the size of your lot.

The key to landscaping for birds is variety. The more diverse the plantings, the more species you will attract. Plant a selection of trees, shrubs, bushes, vines and flowers. The varying heights and densities of these plantings will increase the number of habitats created.

Before you start, draw up a plan and select your plantings and their locations carefully. Choose your sites to maximize the "edge effect." The edge referred to is the boundary between two different habitat types—the border between an open lawn area and a shrubby area for example. The edge effect is an increase in species diversity that occurs because species from both types of habitats can be found along the boundary. Plant trees and shrubs in clumps to provide dense habitat protection from predators and bad weather. Hedgerows can also provide this protection and should be a minimum of ten feet wide. For best results, consult your local garden center for information on plantings that do well in your area. Follow general gardening guidelines, including proper preparation of the ground, cultivation, fertilization and mulching of new plants.

Choose a variety of seed, nut and berry producing trees and shrubs. Different species of birds favor different food sources, so find out what local birds are attracted to. Vines and ground cover also offer food and protection to a number of species, especially ground-feeding birds. Seed eaters will appreciate stands of sunflowers, cosmos, asters and zinnias or other flowers that produce high numbers of seeds. In colder climates, these flowers can be left standing all winter to act as natural bird feeders. Nectar-loving birds, such as the delightful hummingbirds, can be encouraged by a variety of trumpet-shaped flowers, especially red, orange or purple ones. These tiny, energy-packed birds will visit morning glories, honeysuckles, lilies, hollyhocks, jewel-weed and other similar flowers. Hanging baskets on your porch or plantings near a window can bring these birds in very close for an excellent view.

In larger areas it may be possible to leave an old log or tree stump as a site for cavity dwellers. They also provide a habitat for insects, and these will, in turn, attract insect-eating birds such as woodpeckers, nuthatches and creepers.

In addition to providing a variety of natural plantings, you can add some home-made structures to augment the lure of your yard. These projects are ideal for children and can be made with few materials and minimal aid. It brings great satisfaction to children to see a bird nesting in their bird house or feeding at their feeder. They will feel a sense of accomplishment and pride in the fact that they have helped the local wildlife in a small way. Children learn by doing, and having them actively involved in a wildlife project is the best possible way of teaching them that they have an important role to play in conservation.

Building A Bird House

Birds, like people, are fussy about where they will live. Cavity nesters, such as woodpeckers and some ducks, owls and songbirds, will be attracted to a bird house if it meets their standards. Each species has special requirements, so you must decide what you want to attract and then find out in detail what constitutes a suitable nesting box. The important specifications are: entrance hole diameter and height from the floor, floor area, and height of the walls. Once you have built your bird house, you will again need to bow to the vagaries of the species when selecting a spot for it. The height above ground and the type of habitat (near shrubs or in the open) are the two most critical decisions.

The simple design shown here can be adapted to different species of birds.

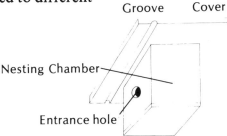

BIRD HOUSE

Materials
- ☐ wood
- ☐ nails and screws
- ☐ glue
- ☐ wood stain

Method
1. Cut the wood to the necessary specifications. You will need: 4 walls, one with the entrance hole; a bottom; a lid; and a cover with a groove cut on the underside. This groove will prevent rain from dripping into the box.
2. Glue or screw lid in the center of the cover's underside.
3. Assemble sides and bottom using nails and glue.
4. Screw the lid to the walls on two sides. This will allow you to remove the lid and cover to clean out the nest box at the end of the nesting season.

5. Stain the outside of the box a dark brown or green to blend in with the natural environment.
6. Mount your box in a suitable location according to the species' requirements. Protect it from cats by installing a sheet metal guard, in the form of an upside down funnel, around the post below the box.

Birds that do not nest in cavities can be attracted to your yard to nest if you supply the required food, water, shelter and nesting materials, such as grass, straw, bark strips, twigs or pieces of string or wool.

Invite a Bird to Dine
In regions where natural food supplies become scarce during part of the year, bird feeders can be welcome additions to any backyard. The birds will set up regular visiting patterns, and you can readily observe them if you locate your feeder near a window. Once you start feeding birds, they will come to rely on you, so be prepared the make the commitment.

There are many different kinds of bird feeders that you can buy, but building one is much more fun, and more economical. Here are the instructions for a simple feeder.

Materials (measurements are approximate)
1. one piece white pine measuring 2 cm x 30 cm x 30 cm (3/4 in. x 12 in. x 12 in.)
2. two pieces white pine measuring 2.5 cm x 2.5 cm x 11 cm (1 in. x 1 in. x 4-1/4 in.)
3. two pieces white pine measuring 2.5 cm x 2.5 cm x 15 cm (1 in. x 1 in. x 6 in.)
4. one piece white pine measuring 2 cm x 25 cm x 25 cm (3/4 in. x 10 in. x 10 in.)
5. four pieces white pine measuring 1.3 cm x 2.5 cm x 2.5 cm (1/2 in. x 1 in. x 1 in.)

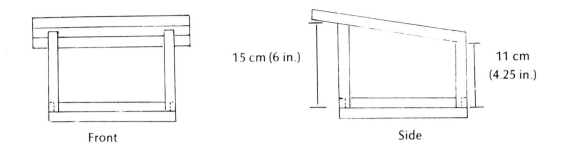

Front

15 cm (6 in.)

11 cm (4.25 in.)

Side

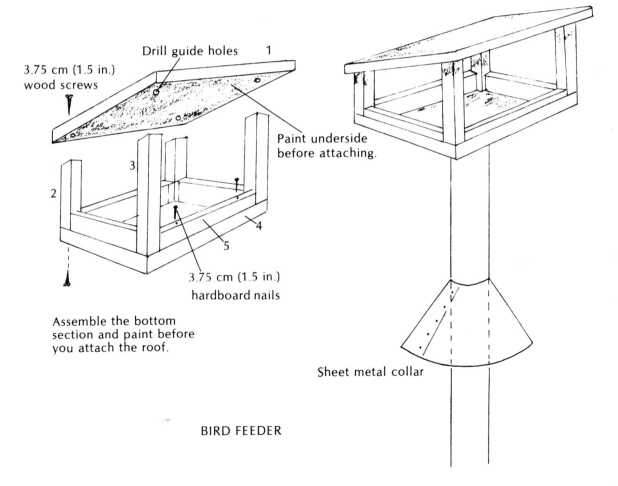

Drill guide holes   1

3.75 cm (1.5 in.)
wood screws

Paint underside
before attaching.

3

2

4

5

3.75 cm (1.5 in.)
hardboard nails

Assemble the bottom
section and paint before
you attach the roof.

Sheet metal collar

BIRD FEEDER

- [ ] eight 3.75 cm (1-1/2 in.) wood screws
- [ ] 3.75 cm (1-1/2 in.) hardboard nails
- [ ] drill to make guide holes for screws
- [ ] stain and brushes

To cut the slant for the roof posts, lay out the side view of your feeder, full size, on a piece of paper. Use the paper pattern to cut the slant.

Your new feeder can be put up in many different ways. Try to place it near bushes or other vegetation, so visiting birds will have some shelter or cover.

What to feed the birds is another important consideration. Different species often prefer different types and sizes of feed, so a safe practice is to offer a good mix to keep everyone happy. You can try varying the mix using these basic ingredients, but the birds will be your best critics.

Wire

Eyelet screen

Suet   Birch log

SUET LOG

Mixed Bird Feed
☐ Hemp	25%
☐ Cereal grasses	25%
☐ Sunflower seeds	25%
☐ Buckwheat	10%
☐ Peanut hearts	10%
☐ Grit (coarse white sand)	5%

Some birds, such as woodpeckers, will be attracted to suet feeders. Suet is made by melting beef fat and then cooling it. It can be placed in chunks on a feeding platform or suspended in mesh bag (such as a vegetable bag) from a branch. You can also make two very simple suet feeders to hang in your yard.

A suet log can be made by drilling 2.5 cm (1 in.) holes, about 2 cm (3/4 in.) deep in short pieces of birch or poplar. The suet is stuffed into the holes and the log is suspended from a branch or pole. A suet cone is easily prepared by rolling large cones from pine or other coniferous trees in warm suet. For an added treat, peanut butter can be added to the suet and the cone can then be rolled in fine seeds. Suspend the cone from a tree branch.

Hummingbirds can be attracted not only by certain flowers, but also by a home-made hummingbird feeder.

Materials
- ☐ clean pop bottle (or similar container)
- ☐ bracket to hold bottle
- ☐ one-holed rubber or cork stopper
- ☐ glass tubing bent at an angle
- ☐ sugar solution

Method
1. Fill the bottle half full with sugar solution and place the stopper in the bottle.
2. Place the glass tubing in the stopper and suspend the bottle upside down, using a bracket.

The hummingbirds will feed by placing their long bill part way into the glass tubing. Locate your hummingbird feeder where you can see it well from a window.

Wire (substituted for bracket)

Wood dowel (substituted for bracket)

Pop bottle

Sugar solution

Cork stopper

Glass tubing

HUMMINGBIRD FEEDER

Feeding Shelter

If you have a large rural property where bigger bird species, such as pheasant or grouse, may be found, a special shelter can attract them for you to observe, as well as provide a reliable feeding station through a cold winter.

Materials
- ☐ saplings
- ☐ rope for lashing
- ☐ pine boughs
- ☐ feed—cracked corn, whole dried ears of corn, seeds

Method
1. Lash saplings into a self-standing frame, as shown.
2. Cut pine boughs and lay them against two sides of the frame, leaving the leeward side open.
3. Spread feed on the ground within the shelter.

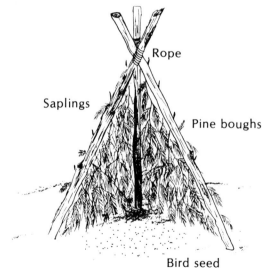

Rope

Saplings

Pine boughs

Bird seed

BIRD SHELTER

44

Bird Baths

Birds will appreciate the addition of a water supply for drinking and bathing. A variety of baths are available commercially, or you can make your own. A simple earthenware pie plate or a flowerpot saucer can be used, providing it has a rough edge, gently sloping sides and a maximum depth of 7.6 cm (3 in.). Place the container in an open area out of reach of neighborhood cats.

Attracting Butterflies and Moths

Butterflies are like winged flowers. Their brilliant colors flitting through the air add beauty and interest to any garden. Most adult butterflies and moths feed on nectar and can therefore be attracted by planting a variety of shrubs, trees and flowers. Suggestions include sumac, blueberry, pussy willow, wild cherry, walnut, larkspur, petunias, 4 o'clocks, marigolds and zinnias.

Adult moths can be attracted, on a temporary basis, to provide a closer look at these night creatures. Many moths have beautiful wing colors and patterns, some with wingspans up to 15 cm (6 in.). Check the undersides of the wings too, as this is often the most attractive side. Two simple methods for attracting moths can be tried.

1. A simple light trap can be set up by hanging an old sheet from the side of a building or from a tree branch, and shining a bright light on it. Moths will be attracted by the light and you will be able to see them at close range.
2. Another method of attracting moths involves mixing up a smelly, sticky mixture of fermented fruit juices, stale beer, mush bananas and molasses or honey, and spreading it on the trunk of a tree in the evening. The odors from the mixture will attract hungry adult moths.

You should also be aware that you may get some bonus visitors, such as beetles, ants, roaches, flies, daddy longlegs, spiders and sowbugs. Lucky you, you can have a whole party of creatures to watch!

Other Wildlife

If you have a rural lot where space is not a problem, you may wish to attract other kinds of wildlife as well. Species that may become a nuisance in an urban setting can be enjoyed in larger areas. Brush piles can be created near the edges of wooded areas for cottontails. Nest boxes for squirrels can be erected in nearby trees at a height of 6 metres (20 feet) above ground. Chipmunks can also be attracted by providing stone piles for cover. A wide variety of creatures can be housed in and under rotting logs, in hollow trees and high grass. If you have the space and enjoy the company, you can create a vibrant and welcoming habitat for a wealth of wildlife.

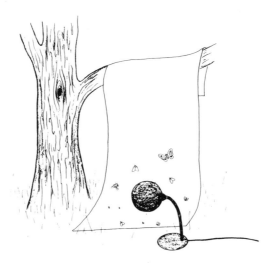

ATTRACTING MOTHS

Observing Wildlife

There are many opportunities to participate in day field trips or more extensive excursions in order to view wildlife. These outings can be geared to specific observations, such as whale watching, or to a more general look into an area's natural history. Tours vary in price and quality, so it is necessary to choose carefully.

There can be a number of advantages to taking a guided trip. Your guide is usually an experienced naturalist who can point out and interpret features that you are not familiar with and that you might overlook. As well, you may get to visit some excellent natural areas that are hidden away or inaccessible to the general public. Well-run trips can introduce you to new areas, fields of interest and skills which can be further developed on your own. A tour can also provide special opportunities and equipment out of the reach of most people. Whale watching, for instance, can be a tremendous experience when shared with professionals who will maximize your enjoyment and learning, as well as ensure your safety.

Such tours are, of course, special events. But wherever you live—even in the heart of a city—you can make nature an important part of your life. The tremendous diversity of animal life and habitats, changing seasons, life cycles and habits all combine to make wildlife observation an intriguing, but challenging, pursuit.

To maximize your success rate and minimize disappointments, you will need good wildlife observation skills. Hints on how to improve your skills can be broken down into four questions: Where to Look? When to Look? What to Look For? and How to Look?

Where to Look?

Wildlife is not restricted to wilderness. Many species inhabit urban and rural areas, some in surprising numbers. It is not necessary to drive for hours just to have contact with nature. Even city parks, ravines, watersheds or backyards can offer limited access to a variety of wildlife. Granted, you will not see a moose or Grizzly Bear in a downtown park, but you often can see birds, insects, squirrels and other small animals that are, in their own way, just as fascinating.

A habitat is the place in which a plant or animal lives. It offers the specific conditions, such as food, water, temperature, light, needed for survival. Habitat requirements are a characteristic of each species and can be used as a general guide to locating individual species. In addition to habitat, a species has a geographic range. Some animals are found in certain areas and not others—usually a result of habitat requirements, but sometimes simply because they have not yet spread that far. When you know a species' habitat and range, you will have a good general idea of where to look for it. This, of course, is only the beginning.

A habitat description can lead you to a very general location, such as a marsh, field or forest. Within each of these large habitats, a myriad of different micro-habitats await discovery. For example, a forest can be home to hundreds of different species. Starting at the bottom, some creatures live in the ground, others on the ground in the leaf litter, some on the small plants, others on shrubs and saplings, and others in the mature trees. It is like a multi-storeyed apartment building, with each unit representing a different micro-habitat.

You do not even need a whole forest to find a variety of micro-habitats. A single tree can host a fascinating array of creatures all on its own. Insects or other invertebrates can be found around the roots, on the bark, under the bark, on and under the leaves, in the flowers or in the wood itself if there is an open wound. Larger animals also inhabit trees. Some birds build nests on the branches, while others excavate a hole in the tree trunk for a nesting cavity. Hollows in trees may be home to squirrels, raccoons, skunks, porcupines or opossums. And when a tree dies and falls to the ground to rot, a whole new selection of residents, from snakes and salamanders to mice and rabbits, may move in.

This is just one of many examples which show the wealth of animal hide-aways that so often go unnoticed. When you are walking through the woods, poke a stick into a rotting stump, turn over a rock to see what may be hiding underneath, and check out the bark or leaves on a tree. Your walk may take longer, but the rewards are endless.

Learn to look for the little places. Get down on your hands and knees and look at a patch of grass or a pile of decaying leaves. See how many different creatures you can find. Introduce children to the secret life of the natural world. But remember to remind them of the need to replace all overturned rocks, logs or other objects as they are found. Respect for the wildlife should be an implicit lesson in all of your observations.

When to Look?

Your observation of wildlife can be affected by two important factors: time of year and time of day. If a species is migratory, it will not be within the same general area all year long. Knowing when a species migrates, and where, can be very helpful in planning your observations. Birds, for instance, have been well studied and their arrival at certain locations can often be predicted with remarkable accuracy.

Even when an animal stays around all year, it is not always readily seen. For example, in colder climates some animals, such as woodchucks and snakes, hibernate during the winter.

Other animals, such as mice and voles, may spend most of their winters in tunnels under the snow, so they are not readily visible either. Turtles and frogs bury themselves in mud on the bottom of their pond, while other water dwellers, like beavers and muskrats, spend much of their winter under ice.

Time of day may also determine what wildlife you can observe. Getting up to watch the sun rise can be a breathtaking experience for a child. But, combined with an early morning hike or a visit to a local field or pond, it can be awe-inspiring. The whole world seems to wake up before your eyes. The birds are chattering even before the sun appears, already busily into the day's routine. The squirrels and chipmunks are dashing here and there and, just like people, many animals are ready for their first meal of the day. Many species take advantage of the cool morning air to feed and move about before the sun gets too hot. The sights and sounds of animals starting their day in their own natural community bring a feeling of harmony and tranquillity. If you are out camping or at your cottage, dawn can also be the best time to escape the human noises of daily living. For many people, this is the time of day when they feel closest to nature.

As the day gets longer, many animals seek shade and rest. For others, though, this is the time to get busy. Since many flowers are only open while the sun is out, nectar-drinking insects and birds do their flower visiting during the day. For some insects, such as butterflies, the sun is like a battery recharger—they rely on it for energy. The sun warms the butterfly's body until it is able to fly. When the insects are out, naturally insect-eaters are also active, and many turtles and snakes bask in the sun on exposed logs or rocks in order to raise their body temperature.

Sunset brings its own performance. Visit a pond or marsh

at dusk and be entertained by the overwhelming chorus of frogs and Spring Peepers. Watch for the V-shaped jet stream in the water, revealing the head of a beaver dragging newly felled branches back to its lodge. As the light fades, you will see less but you can still listen for the various calls of the loon or the loud grump of the bullfrog. And one creature makes seeing it in the dark easy—the little beetle known as a firefly. The flashes of light emitted by its abdomen are a great delight to children.

The possibilities are almost limitless. You may wish to explore all kinds of different habitats, or choose one which you can get to know in more detail. By regularly observing the daily routines of species in a nearby area, a general pattern will emerge. Many species have predictable habits which can be studied and recorded. "Eavesdropping" on wildlife helps a child see the relationships between plants and animals within a community. The various characters in the web of life take on names and faces recognized by an observing child.

What to Look For?

Each habitat has its own mix of species. Some are easy to find and others are elusive. What you *will* see is a variety of shapes, sizes and colors. But even these basic characteristics can change for an individual animal, depending on the stage of its life. Don't forget about eggs, larvae and pupae, as well as adult stages—all are worth a closer look.

Simple identification of animals based on certain characteristics is a good way to develop a child's observational skills. Color, shape and size, habitat and behavior can all be used to identify an animal. It is not important to be able to put a name to each species observed—this may add to enjoyment as expertise is developed, but initially it can be intimidating or frustrating to have to memorize names. Some names will be remembered, others forgotten—the object is for the child to see the differences between animals and realize that a name is only one means of identification.

How to Look?

The answer to this question depends on what you are looking for. Small creatures, like insects or worms, can often be observed at close quarters with little trouble. Children will find that a small magnifying lens attached to a string around their neck will reveal any number of wonders. Familiar sights take on a whole new look at close range. What appears to be a rather dull bug can, under close scrutiny, present an intricate landscape of ridges, hairs, scales, specially designed mouthparts and defense mechanisms.

Bug boxes are also very popular with young children. These small plexiglass boxes have a removable lid with a built in magnifier. This allows the child to pick up a small creature and put it in the box for a short period in order to observe it, larger than life, without having it crawl away.

A great variety of tiny creatures live in the top few centimetres (2 or 3 inches) of soil and in the layer of decaying matter on the ground's surface. This is one of the most active and important zones in the environment. It is here that micro-organisms, insects and other tiny animals and plants break down decaying plant and animal material, releasing nutrients to the soil. These nutrients are, in turn, taken up by growing plants which feed many animals. This is the base of the food web. Even after probing through this zone with your fingers and hand lens, many possible sightings will have eluded you. A simply constructed apparatus, known as a Berlese Funnel, can help children discover these biologically important animals.

Setting Up a Berlese Funnel

Materials
- ☐ wide-mouthed jar
- ☐ large funnel
- ☐ light bulb
- ☐ moistened paper towel
- ☐ trowel
- ☐ paper bag

Method
1. Using your trowel, collect some leaf mold and a bit of top soil from the woods and put it in a paper bag.
2. Transfer the collected materials to the funnel.
3. Place moistened paper towel in the bottom of the jar.

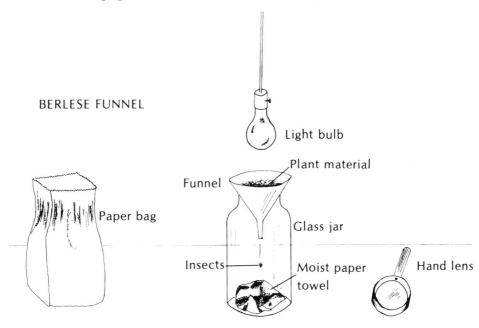

BERLESE FUNNEL

Light bulb

Plant material

Funnel

Paper bag

Glass jar

Insects

Moist paper towel

Hand lens

4. Place the funnel in the mouth of the jar and lower the light bulb over the funnel. The heat and light from the bulb will cause the moisture-loving creatures to dig farther through the leaf litter, and they will eventually drop out of the funnel into the jar below.
5. After one or two hours, check the jar regularly for specimens. Observe them with a hand lens and then release them.

Marsh Miniatures

Similarly, there are simple techniques for discovering many aquatic invertebrates (animals without backbones, such as insects and crustaceans). Invertebrates provide food for a variety of other marsh dwellers, such as fish, amphibians, reptiles and birds. Even though many are not readily visible, they are a very important part of the marsh's food web and, therefore, deserve a closer look.

With some very basic equipment, you can launch a close-up investigation of the secret wildlife in a marsh and discover some of the reasons why wetlands are among the most important ecosystems in nature.

For an initial glimpse, make a simple water scope from a tall, wide-mouthed glass jar, such as a pickle jar. Take off the lid and lower the jar into water, bottom first, until water level is about two or three centimetres (an inch) below the open end of the jar. Do not allow water to enter the jar. Bend over and look inside the jar, through the glass bottom and sides, to see what is moving underwater.

For more thorough observation, you can make some simple marsh probes.

Materials

☐ shallow pan, preferably with light-colored bottom
☐ pail or bucket for collecting samples
☐ insect net made from broom handle, coat hanger and old nylons or muslin, for sweeping the vegetation along the shore (not for use in the water)
☐ screen made with fiberglass window screen stretched and stapled between two wooden handles, for catching specimens in the water
☐ kitchen strainer tied to broom handle to provide a longer reach for catching aquatic creatures
☐ kitchen baster and camel hair brush for transferring specimens
☐ small, clear bottles, such as rinsed pill bottles
☐ field guides
☐ rubber gloves—useful when water is cold
☐ magnifying glass

Method

1. Fill your shallow pan with clear water. This will be your Observation Post.
2. Using strainers and screens, dip into the water to catch any invertebrates that are swimming around. Move the strainer horizontally through the vegetation, with the open side facing in the direction in which you are moving it. Gently jiggle it along the vegetation, looking for the creatures that fall free. Carefully transfer any creatures to the Observation Post using your fingers or a camel hair brush. Also check the leaves of floating vegetation and on the stems of emergent vegetation.
3. Take a bottom sample using the pail. Transfer a piece of muck to the sieve and bob it up and down in the water to

wash away the silt, being careful to always keep the rim above water. Look for the specimens left behind and transfer them to the Observation Post.

4. For a closer look at a specimen, use the baster to transfer it from the large pan into an individual jar filled with water (leave air space at top). This jar can be closely observed to provide a first rate view of the tiny wetland animal.

5. A magnifying glass will enable you to see the invisible life that teems in fresh water.

6. Using your insect net, sweep through the shoreline vegetation to see what hopping, flying or crawling insects are hidden there.

When you find a specimen, notice its color, size, shape, number of legs, how it travels and what part of the marsh it came from. Check your field guides for identification, or make sketches of those that cannot be identified and look them up later. Try to find out what each specimen feeds on and what it is, in turn, eaten by. Remember—return all specimens to their original location when the investigation is finished.

Simple activities like these can be easily repeated. By keeping records of their observations, children can find out if the number and kinds of creatures differ from area to area or even through the year. Keeping a nature notebook not only helps a child remember different experiences, but also allows for year-to-year comparisons of observations. In fact, biologists rely on their field notes to help determine population trends, changes in habitat quality and many other factors which are necessary in predicting the need for wildlife management.

Using a Blind
As a general rule, the larger the wildlife, the farther away you must be to observe it. This is where technical aids, such as

binoculars and telescopes, can make your efforts easier and often more fruitful. Common sense tells you that if you want wildlife to make an appearance, you have to be quiet and unobtrusive. Young children, however, may find these rules too confining, in which case a new approach is needed. Just as animals have special ways of camouflaging themselves, people, too, can devise ways to keep out of sight.

Blinds are small, covered structures designed to hide people and equipment from nearby wildlife. Commonly used by hunters and photographers, a blind allows people to watch wildlife without frightening it. There are many different kinds of blinds: some are built on land, others float on the water and still others are built up in trees. You can construct a simple blind and increase your opportunities for wildlife viewing.

A basic construction involves canvas or burlap (a neutral color is best) draped over four upright posts, or three posts lashed together tipi style. The blind should be one and a half to two metres (5-6 feet) high, with enough ground area to suit your needs. It is very important that there be no loose ends of material which may flap around and scare the wildlife. Another form of blind is the umbrella blind. Fasten an open umbrella to a stake or hollow aluminium pole. Plant the pole securely in the ground at the chosen location. Attach a cloth around the edge of the umbrella to create a tent, and weigh down the edges with pegs, rocks or logs. Viewing holes should be cut at appropriate heights all around the blind to increase your range of observation.

A more natural looking blind can be built with poles lashed together in a lean-to fashion and covered with pine or cedar boughs on three sides. This is essentially a scaled-up version of the feeding shelter described earlier.

Even when you are out of sight, wildlife may not appear right away. By studying the area for a few days you should be able to determine the best location for your blind and the best times to use it. If there is a bird's nest nearby, for example, you may want to set up your blind so that you can observe the mother feeding her young. Because you will be hidden, your presence will not be disturbing and you will be treated to some wonderful sights. Even so, it is wise to provide a comfortable seat in your blind and perhaps some quiet busy-work for young children while you wait for the wildlife to appear.

Tips on Photographing Wildlife
Simple wildlife photography can bring a lot of pleasure to children and improve their observation skills at the same time. Although professionals use expensive and specialized equipment to achieve their high quality products, even a basic camera can be put to good use with a little planning.

Obviously, one of the first steps to photographing wildlife is to get a subject. This can be facilitated by setting up simple backyard lures to attract different animals. Find out what species of wildlife are found locally and what kinds of habitat or food will draw them to your yard. For instance, a bird feeder will attract a variety of birds to your location. If you position yourself nearby, hidden in a blind, you will be able to focus on the feeder or a nearby branch and wait for the perfect picture. Putting nuts or seeds out in an area with a nice background may entice squirrels or chipmunks into your outdoor "studio."

Some favorite subjects, such as butterflies, are difficult to capture on film in the wild. However, if you raise a butterfly from a caterpillar or chrysalis, you will have a perfect subject to photograph. Insects are less active on cool, dull days, and therefore your chances of finding one relatively motionless may be improved on such days.

Although the best shots are sometimes the product of long hours of patient waiting, if you always have the camera ready, you can take advantage of chance sightings. In addition, try taking pictures at different times of the day or night. You can record the variety of species in your neighborhood and learn a lot about their habitats and habits through your observations.

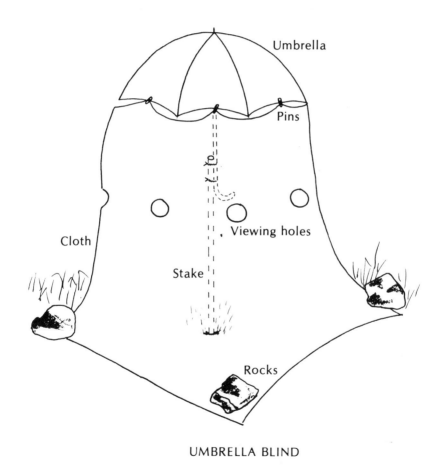

Umbrella

Pins

Viewing holes

Cloth

Stake

Rocks

UMBRELLA BLIND

More than Meets the Eye

The natural environment is a fascinating treasure trove of sights, smells, tastes, textures and sounds. Although sight is the predominantly used sense, other senses can be stimulated and developed for the interpretation of your surroundings. As each sense is used more frequently, the outdoor experience is enriched and often becomes more memorable.

Children are well-suited to a number of activities that heighten their sensitivity to natural smells, sounds and textures. Try some of these activities. Awaken the senses to the essence of nature. Extend your vision.

Sound

Listening to nature can not only reveal the voices of unseen creatures, but can also introduce the sounds of the habitat itself. Water rippling in a brook, breezes rustling through the grass or rain falling gently on the leaves—all represent another expression of the natural environment.

Take children out to a meadow, lie down on your back and listen. Set a time limit of, say, two minutes. After the time is up, ask them to tell you everything they have heard and write it down. Do the same thing in a woods and by a stream or pond. Compare your notes and talk about the different kinds of sounds in each area.

The sounds of nature can be likened to a form of music. Each habitat has its own "orchestra" and favorite theme song. Can you distinguish any of the players? Try to pick out the different voices of birds as they chase each other across invisible territorial boundaries. The droning of bees and buzzing of insects will add another dimension to your attuned ears. As will the odd mosquito bite!

Sounds seem to be magnified in the dark. As your vision becomes less reliable, your other senses begin to take over, opening the door for a new range of experiences. When you are out at dusk catching the evening display, stay a bit later. As darkness progresses, the air fills with a host of new sounds, some soothing and others spine tingling. An owl's baritone, the laugh-like call of a loon or the high-pitched howling of wolves can set a child's imagination on fire. Becoming familiar with the sounds of the night can increase a child's enjoyment of nature as well as ease a fear of the dark. Just knowing what's out there can make the night friendlier.

Recording nature sounds can be a whole new hobby in itself. If you have access to a tape recorder, start with some of the louder, more noticeable sounds, such as an evening serenade of frogs or a waterfall. Children can have a lot of fun experimenting with different sounds. You can make up games using your tape recorder and having children guess what made a particular sound.

Professional nature recorders have more sophisticated equipment, including parabolas and other devices designed to heighten the sound experience. Many nature recordings are available commercially and may be a great source of enjoyment and relaxation for all ages. Close your eyes, turn on the sounds, and let your imagination take you to the wilds. Some records are designed to teach the recognition of nature sounds; the most popular of these are the bird recordings. As a child's interest in identifying species grows, these aids may be useful.

Smell
Although you may not have realized it, smells have played an important role in your interpretation and enjoyment of situations and places, and often figure prominently in your memories of events. You have only to think of the wonderful

freshness in the air after rainfall or the fragrance of newly opened blossoms to be grateful for your sense of smell.

The ability to smell things allows animals, including people, to discover and identify things that can be neither seen nor heard. Many animals rely on their keen sense of smell for survival, detecting the presence of danger by scents carried in the air. You need only observe a dog walking through unfamiliar territory to see how important smell is. Other animals use odor as a defense mechanism. In particular, mammals belonging to the Mustelidae family, which includes mink and skunks, are well equipped with anal scent glands. As you probably know, it does not take long to find out if a skunk feels threatened.

People, too, use their sense of smell in daily activities, but it is not as keenly developed as an animal's and it is often taken for granted. But children can be taught to be more attentive to smells. Get them to go outside, close their eyes and smell the air. What can be identified? Perhaps the scents of garden flowers, newly mown grass, or something cooking on a barbeque. By interpreting these urban scents, a child can figure out some of the activities that have recently taken place in the neighborhood. A rural setting may reveal a whole new range of smells—domestic animals, manure, freshly cut hay . . . all are clues to the surrounding environment.

The same activity can be tried in a natural setting. This time a child can be asked to describe the scents using words: sweet, damp, fresh, decaying, perfume-like. Once a list has been made, the child can play detective and try to discover the sources of the various smells.

Another popular game involves the collection of small pieces of different natural materials. At first you may wish to include some familiar smells, such as garlic, onion, or a well-known flower, so youngsters are able to correctly guess a few of the samples. This gives the game a positive start and reinforces the concept that smell alone can be used to successfully identify things. Once the materials are arranged, the players must close their eyes, smell each object, without touching it, and try to name it. You can help by giving clues about where you found it, what color it is and so on. This game can be played anywhere and anytime with minimal preparation. Try it in different habitats and refer to it often. An increased sensitivity to the natural world will be a valued gift for years to come.

Touch
Touching is another way of discovering your surroundings—it is more intimate and brings you closer to nature. Try a variant of the smelling game, this time emphasizing the sense of touch. Gather an assortment of blunt, sharp, wet, dry, hairy, sticky and slimy specimens to tantalize a child's newly awakening sense. See how many objects can be identified by feel alone. In some cases, the feel of an animal can be a clue to its general identity. For instance, amphibians have moist skin whereas reptiles have a dry covering.

The identification of many plants can also be aided by touch. There is an almost limitless variety of textures in nature. Even a single plant can offer an amazing diversity of tactile experiences. For example, the stem, leaves, bud, flower, seeds and roots can be distinctly different. It is wise to do some research beforehand, in order to determine the identity of any local plants that should be avoided. You would not want a child fingering poison ivy, poison oak or stinging nettles—nor do you really want to touch them yourself.

A Trust Walk
An excellent way of experiencing nature without seeing it is to

go on a Trust Walk. Children can be blindfolded and led by the hand on a short walk through a field or woods. Initially this may be an intimidating experience, so walk slowly and carefully, and reassure the children that you will not leave. After a few minutes, stop and let go, but do not leave. Ask them to describe the spot where they are standing. Encourage them to touch the ground and surrounding vegetation, to describe the smells and sounds of the area. Ask them to imagine and tell you what the spot looks like. Take off the blindfold and reveal the area—how does vision affect their interpretation of the surroundings? This experience can be repeated in different areas and the walk can be extended as the participants gain confidence.

All of these activities are designed to strengthen a child's awareness of natural surroundings and develop an appreciation for what cannot be seen.

Be a Wildlife Detective

Many wildlife species avoid human contact. For children, this can be a disappointing reality, and their enthusiasm for wildlife viewing can dissipate rather quickly unless a new tack is taken. Although you may not see a deer or porcupine on your hike through the woods, you may be able to find out where they have been by checking for tracks, clipped vegetation and other signs that tell the secrets of wildlife inhabitants.

By learning some of the more visible wildlife clues, your children can turn into detectives, stooping and snooping along the trail on a personal animal investigation. The following is a brief guide to detecting unseen creatures on your outings.

Get Tracking
Finding and identifying animal tracks can be a lot of fun, as well as a good way to learn more about local wildlife populations. There are several good guides to animal tracks available in libraries and bookstores.

Important features to note when identifying a track include:

☐ size of front and hind tracks
☐ location (habitat)
☐ shape of track (paw-like, cloven-hoofed, and so on)
☐ evidence of claws
☐ relative position of the tracks
☐ depth of the tracks (can indicate size and weight of animal)
☐ evidence of a tail track

Many good tracks can be found in soft, moist earth, especially along the banks of streams or ponds where animals come to drink, leaving tell-tale prints in the mud. As well, areas of snow can offer excellent opportunities to view animal tracks.

Track Casting

Making plaster casts of animal tracks is a relatively simple and interesting hobby for children. Plaster casts can provide a permanent record of local wildlife without any danger to the animals. In fact, you do not even have to see the animals. Follow these simple instructions and introduce children to a new way of observing wildlife that may develop into an exciting new pastime.

When you have demonstrated the technique once or twice, let the child try it alone. With a little practice, excellent casts can be produced and a proud collection started.

Materials
- ☐ plain plaster of Paris (available at most hardware stores)— about 1 kg (2 lbs.) in a tightly sealed container
- ☐ container of water
- ☐ a thin plastic container for mixing
- ☐ a stick for stirring
- ☐ cardboard strips 2-3 cm (about 1 in.) wide and 10-50 cm (4-20 in.) long
- ☐ wire (optional)
- ☐ newspaper
- ☐ field notebook and pencil

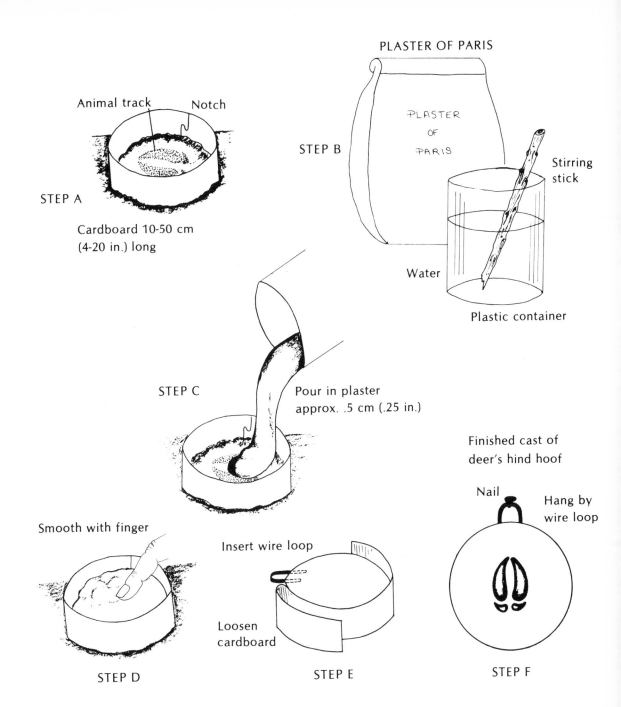

Animal track   Notch

STEP A

Cardboard 10-50 cm
(4-20 in.) long

PLASTER OF PARIS

PLASTER OF PARIS

STEP B

Stirring stick

Water

Plastic container

STEP C   Pour in plaster
approx. .5 cm (.25 in.)

Finished cast of
deer's hind hoof

Smooth with finger

Insert wire loop

Nail   Hang by
wire loop

Loosen
cardboard

STEP D   STEP E   STEP F

Method

1. Once you have located a clear track in the ground, make a cardboard ring out of one of the strips by notching its ends together. Fit the ring around the track and press firmly.
2. Roughly estimate the amount of plaster needed. Pour one-third of this amount into the plastic mixing container. Add water and stir gently with a stick until the mixture is smooth and the consistency of pablum or oatmeal. If it is too thin, add more plaster.
3. Using the stick, hit the side of the mixing container a few times in order to get air bubbles to rise to the surface and break.
4. Slowly pour the plaster mixture into the track until it almost fills the cardboard ring. Leave about a 1/2 cm (1/4 in.) space at the top.
5. Smooth the surface of the plaster with a stick or finger, and let it set for 20 to 30 minutes. Clean off your equipment since plaster sets quickly. During the waiting period young naturalists can look for more tracks or fill in information in a field notebook. Do not forget to record the location, date and name of the animal, if known. Deductions can often be made from spacing, patterns of prints and other clues, allowing you to record whether the track was made by a front or hind foot and whether the animal was walking, running or resting.
6. If you wish, when the cast is semi-hard insert a wire loop for hanging.
7. When the plaster is hard, loosen the cardboard and lift the cast up. Wrap it in newspaper for the trip home. At home, gently wash the mud and dirt from the cast using water and an old toothbrush.
8. The plaster casts can be painted if desired.

Hints
- ☐ A pinch of salt can be added to the dry plaster before mixing. It will speed up the hardening of the cast.
- ☐ Instead of a cardboard collar, you can use collars cut from tin cans, but be careful of the sharp edges. Coating the inside of the tin with vaseline will allow the cast to slip out easily after it has hardened.

Scat and Pellets

The scat (fecal waste) left by animals is a useful clue to an individual's identity. Biologists also use droppings to determine the health of the animal, local population and local diet. Often, remains, such as bones and hair, can be distinguished in the droppings of carnivores. The characteristic size, shape, pattern and color of droppings are all important clues. Check for scat, not only along the trail, but in hollow stumps, caves or other shelters which look like suitable resting spots or residences for wildlife. Sometimes the combination of scat plus tracks is necessary for more accurate identification of an animal.

Some birds, such as owls and hawks, will eat their prey whole, but are unable to digest everything. Instead of excreting the indigestible elements through droppings, these birds regurgitate feathers, bones and fur in neat little packages called pellets or castings. These dry pellets can be very helpful in studying the diet of certain species. However, since the pellets vary according to the kind of food eaten, they are best used in conjunction with other evidence, such as known nest or perch, when identifying a bird. You can dissect an owl pellet and try to identify the tiny skulls, bones, teeth or feathers that you find. Place the pellet in warm water with detergent and let it soak for at least an hour. Put the softened pellet on blotting paper and try to separate its contents using tweezers and needles. It is like a real life jigsaw puzzler.

Gnawings, Borings and Scratchings

Different wildlife species can be distinguished by the characteristic way in which they eat. The gnaw marks on the bark and branch tips of shrubs and trees can prove to be important evidence for wildlife detectives. When you are on a hike, look for some of these signs and you may discover a lot more local wildlife that you were ever aware of.

A familiar sign of a beaver is the leftover stumps of felled trees. A close look will reveal the imprints of this lumberjack's two large incisors. Although both deer and rabbits share a wooded habitat and eat similar foods, you can tell which one has been feeding in a particular spot by looking at the clipped ends of the branches. A rabbit's sharp incisors will neatly bite off the succulent branch tip at a sharp angle. On the other hand, the deer will leave a ragged, torn edge because it does not have any top front teeth with which to bite cleanly.

Several species of mammals, including porcupines, mice, pocket gophers, cottontails and beavers, will gnaw the bark off branches in a distinctive pattern. In colder climates, porcupines will often retreat up a tree for a considerable period during the winter. They feed on the soft inner bark of the branches and twigs, as well as buds. Since the gnaw marks are so high up in the tree, it is unlikely you will be able to observe them. However, if you watch for masses of clipped evergreen branches and scat beneath the tree, you will know that a porcupine has been there (or perhaps still is).

Red Squirrels are messy eaters, leaving ample clues as to their whereabouts. In the fall, these active little creatures will feed on pine cones, stripping the bracts off to get at the seeds. Check rocks, tree stumps and the ground beneath pines for these naked cones.

Bears have their own way of leaving records of their activities. As part of the feeding process, bears will bite and tear off bark strips from the trunks of pine, spruce and fir trees. Then, using their incisors, they scrape off the syrupy substance on the wood and leave behind vertical tooth marks. Other bear clues may be left by young Black Bears climbing soft, smooth-barked trees such as aspen. The claw marks leave wounds in the bark which are eventually transformed into permanent scars. Some bears will choose a tree or stump as a regular scratching post. By backing up to the tree on its hind legs and rubbing vigorously up and down, the bear scratches itself, often leaving scraps of hair stuck to the oozing sap or the bark. It is thought that these scratching posts may also serve as territorial markings and challenges to rivals.

Home Sweet Home

One of the easiest ways to confirm the presence of an animal without actually seeing it is by finding its home. Animal homes come in all shapes, sizes and locations. They can be located in the ground, on the ground, underwater, floating on the water, inside a tree or on its branches.

Beaver lodges and muskrat houses are common wetland sights and are easily recognized by children. Many animals are cavity dwellers, including porcupines, raccoons, owls, woodpeckers, some ducks and other birds, squirrels and opossums. Look for cavities in trees or wooden posts and hollow trunks or stumps.

Other animals prefer to make their homes by burrowing into the ground. Look for the holes of chipmunks, woodchucks, various mice, moles, prairie dogs, weasels and skunks. Sometimes a burrow that has been engineered by one species is used by another. In colder areas, for example, snakes may den up in a mammal's burrow to escape the winter.

One of the most reliable signs of bird life is a nest. Nest watching is a challenging and fascinating hobby that can be

Blue Heron nest.

launched at an early age. Because birds are very sensitive during breeding season, great care must be taken not to disturb the nest or the young. If you are careful, though, you can study a nest over a season and watch as the young hatch, grow and fledge. The intimate relationship between young and adult(s) is a key survival factor. Keep a daily journal of observations, describing the activities at the nest. If you have a camera, some photographs of the nest and young at different stages of development would be an excellent addition to the diary. Make notes on feeding behavior, daily routines, defense mechanisms, changes in appearance of the young and any other interesting observations.

Some birds, particularly those of the woodpecker family—which includes woodpeckers, flickers and sapsuckers—leave bore holes in trees in the course of feeding. The Pileated Woodpecker, one of the largest in this group, may leave groups of very large holes—up to 30 centimetres (12 inches) long—in a tree trunk while searching for a meal of ants. Sapsuckers also leave distinctive pits, often square or oblong, in neat rows on tree trunks or branches.

As you can see, a close look at tree trunks and branches may reveal a number of surprising finds.

Photo Credits: Bill Ivy

Goldfinch nest.

A variety of nests can be found after the breeding season is over, when they have been abandoned and are easy to see. Thus, the location, identification and study of nests is actually a year-round pastime for all to enjoy.

Like birds, nests come in different shapes, sizes and locations. For example, a nest may be in a shrub or tree, on the ground, in the ground, hanging, semi-hanging or perched on rocky ledges or cliffs. Nesting materials also vary, and include sticks, mosses, lichens, grasses, mud, feathers, bark, straw and rootlets. We have illustrated a few common nests to get you started.

By this time, you will see that there is much more to studying wildlife that simple eye contact. Learn to recognize the many different signs left by unseen wildlife and turn every hike into a detective's dream.

Where to Learn More

Having stimulated children's interest in wildlife, you should be prepared to nurture and sustain the interest as they grow older. There are many different resources available to the public, many of which are geared to youth.

Most metropolitan areas have a range of facilities which can supplement a child's exposure to wildlife. A zoo can be an excellent place for youngsters to view wildlife that would otherwise be impossible to see. By visiting a zoo you can be introduced to animals from far away places, see rare or endangered species or catch a glimpse of animals that normally avoid human contact. All of these experiences can be exciting and educational. Zoo visits can be repeated several times with a different theme or objective each time. For example, you may visit species of a particular continent or species belonging to the same family or class. Phone ahead and find out what interpretive programs, if any, are offered. You can use the zoo as an excellent opportunity to get close to wildlife, study it and enjoy it. By planning your visits instead of just wandering randomly among the exhibits, you can get the most out of time spent at the zoo.

A natural history museum is another good place to share with children. Although the specimens are not alive, there is usually an effort to illustrate the animal's natural habitat as well as some behavioral characteristics. These facilities may also offer a fantastic opportunity to view extinct and prehistoric animals. Much can be learned about why some species have died out while others have been able to adapt. For some children, prehistoric life is as intriguing as the thought of extra-terrestrial beings.

If you do not have access to these facilities, there are still many opportunities from which your child can benefit.

Meeting other youngsters who share a fascination with wildlife and the desire to explore nature further can be a very rewarding experience. There are various wildlife and naturalists' associations throughout North America. They range from local to regional to national, and many offer special memberships to families, students and children. Before joining an organization, make sure you understand and agree with its objectives and are aware of what your membership fee will be used for. Many excellent publications, field trips and other benefits arise from affiliation with these groups. To find out about the opportunities available to you, an up-to-date listing of groups is available from two sources:

☐ Canadian Conservation Directory, published by Canadian Nature Federation, Suite 203, 75 Albert St., Ottawa, Ontario, Canada   K1P 6G1.

☐ Conservation Directory, published by National Wildlife Federation, 1412 Sixteenth St. N.W., Washington, D.C. 20036, U.S.A.

If there is nothing available locally, perhaps you and your friends could start your own club or series of natural history outings for children. For advice, or possible help, contact park staff, science teachers and anyone else you can think of who may share your interests.

Youth groups and camps may also be a valuable learning opportunity. Many of these offer a natural history theme and introduce children to new ideas and techniques for enjoying the outdoors and to new, related hobbies.

Libraries can be treasure troves of books and other publications related to wildlife. Children can explore their interests and develop their reading skills at the same time. Consider starting a home library on wildlife or general nature-related topics. The *Nature's Children* Series is an excellent base on which to build. Books can last a lifetime and brings hours of enjoyment through the years.

Getting To Know...

Nature's Children

INDEX

Index

HERBIVORES
HIBERNATORS

Hibernation refers to a state into which some animals go in winter, during which their body temperature is lowered and their breathing and their heart rate slow. Animals in hibernation need very little energy to stay alive.

Some animals, such as bears, which are sometimes thought of as hibernators, do not fall into this category, since their metabolism does not undergo any major changes. Even though they may be less active in winter, they are not in hibernation.

Cold-blooded animals can also be said to hibernate if they remain inactive during the winter. However, unlike warm-blooded animals, their state is brought on by their environment, not by independent metabolic changes in the animal.

If no asterisk appears then all members hibernate; if an asterisk appears then only specific species hibernate.

HUMMINGBIRDS—27

MIGRATORS

  Migration refers to a regular seasonal pattern of travelling, usually in search of food. For the animals listed below, all members migrate, unless an asterisk appears, in which case only some particular species migrate.

Printed and Bound in S¡